as one sees the sun

Rachel Miracle

Presentation by *BookLeaf Publishing*

Web: www.bookleafpub.com

E-mail: info@bookleafpub.com

ISBN: 9789360940690

First edition 2024

For my shooting star, my muse and the light in the dark. For the little shards of hope I find along my journey that keep me going. And for you. If you needed a sign, this is it. Don't give up.

ACKNOWLEDGEMENT

Thank you for taking the time to read this. We write for ourselves but it's in the interpretations of our works that we are immortalized.

PREFACE

Something I've thought about quite a few times before is the circumstance of falling stars. For us, they are gifts, bestowed into our open hands. They are magnificent presentations of hope. We tie our dreams to them. When we're swimming in adversity, it's the wishes they let us make that pull us out of the water. And yet, in direct juxtaposition, for them to be taken from their rightful place in the sky just to crash to earth.. To relocate to a place so thick with suffering.. What a punishment that must be. They save us and in return, we doom them. The contrast of blessing and curse astounds me. I am humbled by their sacrifice.

Saudade

My love, with me-
Your body was Appalachia
Your pussy a wild flower blooming in a starlit
holler
Your tits were the bountiful Blue Ridge
Mountains decorating your horizon
My fingers were the birch trees along your old
dirt roads
And my tongue was the cloudless sky above
your rolling bluegrass hills
Where you were milkweed decorating the vast
Kentucky fields
And the elk drinking from the deep lake at
Massanetta Springs
I was the Shenandoah river rushing through your
valleys and carving out your landscape
I miss you
I miss you so much

Amore mío, con me-
Your body was the Amalfi coast
Your pussy a hidden cave on the island of Capri
Your tits were Postifino rising up the cliffs from
the sea

My fingers were ships coming to dock at your
port
And my tongue was a cliff diver plunging to
your depths
Where you were brightly colored buildings
hovering over the marina
And the sandy white sun soaked beaches of the
shore
I was the untamable Mediterranean Sea that
caressed you
Mi manchi
Mi manchi tanto

Mon amour, avec moi-
Your body was the Louvre
Your pussy was the Mona Lisa and St. Francis of
Assisi Recieving Stigmata
Your tits were the Venus de Milo and the
Winged Victory of Samothrace
My fingers were on a guided tour, eyes wide,
awestruck and humbled
And my tongue was a thirsty touriste hiding a
camera in the pocket of her coat
And where you were the pillars of the Salle Du
Manège
And the wooden crucifix made of poplar and
pine

I was the curious security guard with his
flashlight trained on the painting of Julienne and
Gabrielle d'Estrées
Tu me manque
Tu me manques tellement

Watashi no ai, watashitoisshoni-
Your body was the city of Tokyo
Your pussy was the Meiji Shinto Shrine with its
towering gate and encircling woods
Your tits were the cherry blossom gardens of
Shinjuku Gyoen
My fingers were the monorails snaking through
your landscape
And my tongue was a Sumidagawa firework
bursting in your sky
Where you were kabuki theaters and Ichiriki
teahouses
Neon skyscrapers and Harajuku fashion displays
I was a geisha bowing at the feet of her most
honorable danna
Anata ga inakute sabishīdesu
Anata ga koishī

Habibti, maei-
Your body was the Valley of the Kings
Your pussy was the east valley in which were
situated countless royal tombs,

Your tits were the pyramids of Giza, regal
against the sand
My fingers were the cobras, vipers and asps
snaking through your crevices
And my tongue was a sandstorm licking at your
walls
Where you were the limestone statue of the
reclining Great Sphinx
And the temples decorating the banks of the Nile
I was Howard Carter, lantern in hand,
dumbstruck at the entrance to Tutankhamun's
tomb
aftaqadk
'aftaqiduk kthyran

mi amor, conmigo-
Your body was the Caribbean island of the
Dominican Republic
Your pussy was the Cibao Valley, rich with rice,
coffee and cacao
Your tits were Cordillera Central, running
through the heart of Hispaniola
My fingers were the Mangroves of Los Haitises
National Park
And my tongue was a tropical cyclone dancing
along your southern coast
Where you were the metropolitan expanse of
what was once Santo Domingo de Guzmán

And the Yaque del Norte emptying into the
Monte Christi Bay
I was the rare bayahiba rose blooming amongst
your thorns
Te extraño
Te extraño mucho

When can I return..?
Quando posso tornares..?
Quand puis-je revenir..?
Itsu kaeremasu ka..?
Mataa yumkinuni aleawdatu..?
Cuándo puedo volver..?

Auspice

encased in an ethereal shade, the harbinger goes

along the quivering horizon of the morning she
slides

into oblivion steps the spellbound fool that
strolls

ephemeral and fleeting, the damage resides

along the quivering horizon of the morning she
slides

the haunting murmur of warning rests at parted
lips

ephemeral and fleeting, the damage resides

hiraeth; the longing for a home that doesn't exist

the haunting murmur of warning rests at parted
lips

It is profound the way the light escapes her from
within

hiraeth; the longing for a home that doesn't exist

saudade; the longing to be near something again

It is profound the way light escapes her from
within

a sparkling effervescence of rich intricacies
apropos

saudade; the longing to be near something again

encased in an ethereal shade, the harbinger goes

burn

you are exceptionally strong willed

but I place an even pressure on your thigh

and I know that you'll give in tonight

you'll park outside your apartment

turn down the stereo

crack the window

so the snowflakes can sneak inside

the thrill of getting caught

makes you feel alive

and without a seconds hesitation

your hand slips down to its destination

you find me

stroke me

trace me

hold me

but there's no time to waste

your trembling fingers

can't bring me

to your mouth fast enough taste

your tongue is wet for release

your body aches to be pleased

but you're struggling to light me up

it takes a few flicks to to do the trick

then I slide easily between your lips

you've craved me

can't break me

you need this fix

suck me in

again

again

let me plant my disease

let my infection spread all through you

infiltrate your lungs

let me destroy you

but i won't be able to last

i'll crumble away in your hands

one breath at a time I'll reduce to ash

but before you toss me away

take another fucking drag, okay?

i'll wrap my hands around your throat

take away your self control

and you'll pretend you're fine alone

but you'll come back for more

and I'll be waiting

where you left me

when you were coming down

in your pocket

in your glove compartment

in the floorboard of your car

wherever you chose to hide me

i'm ready to burn when you are

moonflower & morning glory

i drag my hand down your abdomen
and when i touch you
you realease your breath
not realizing you've been holding it
you're acutely aware of the pressure
and my lips
sliding along your throat
my teeth occasionally biting
pulling at your flesh
you were blissful before
in my arms
but when i give in
and let two fingers slip inside of you
you are euphoriac
you growl with pleasure
bend your head back as i move into a rhythm
outside the tent
the ocean waves crash
and the leaves of the hardy palms
shake with the late night summer wind
the crickets hidden in the brush sing softly in the
darkness
none of that matters to us
we move together in synchronized passion
your arms wrapped loosely around my shoulders

your hips rising and falling to meet my hand
between your legs
with every passing second we come closer to the
end
but in these hungry moments
at least temporarily
we are able to forget
still daybreak creeps up on the campsite softly
the sun sneaking over the horizon
i'm the first to wake up
experiencing the flood of memories of the night
before
i lay, reeling, on my pallet
your beautiful head still resting on my chest
breathing easily, in and out
soon you'll be half a world away
i move one hand to your bare back
let my fingertips trace your spine
you make a small sound, stirring at my touch
you place your lips against the skin of my throat
your kisses are soft and warm
anxiety melts away
i focus on the growing heat between my legs
i catch your face
look into your honey eyes
glittering in the rays of the morning sun
you look innocent, your pink lips pouting
your eyebrows furrowed with worry

your voice is a whisper above the backdrop of
the beach
"i don't want it to end"
my thumbs are brushing your cheeks,
affectionately
your lips are on mine
and my heart is fluttering restlessly in my chest
even in the golden stillness of the morning
you mold perfectly against me
and as we tumble in freefall towards your
inevitable departure
we lose our hold on reality
clinging to our final moments
clinging to one another

roast

i peel my clothes off like string cheese

from a transparent plastic wrapper

and i let them fall in the floor

so that i can trip over them later

and wonder why i do the things i do

and why things have ended up the way they have

and my skin thaws

and my skin blooms with cold chills

only cured when i wrap my towel

around my body like a tortilla

around shredded beef and mozarella cheese

to stand there

to wait there

pushing my hair out of my eyes

like a tray of fries

to the back of the oven shelf

while i let the water warm up

while i let the steam simmer my skin

while i sink in and let the boiling liquid

cook me 'til i'm done

and with my palms i marinade in soup

and with my fingernails i tenderize

the meat of my scalp

with a bouquet of fruity shampoo

only pausing to notice the bruises

like dark spots on potatoes

that must be carved out

like soft brown patches on peaches

that you must eat around

will you eat around?

will you sip me like thin soup

will you place handfuls of me into your wet
mouth

and munch as if i were popcorn

will you lick me off your fingers like barbeque
sauce

will you suck my sweetness from your skin like
caramel

or will you devour me fully

like a meal

like meat nestled beside starches

and followed by the most delicious dessert

that you've ever tasted

or are you even hungry?

Can I?

There's a right way to do this

But I don't give a damn

I want to feel you tighten

Around the fingers of my hand

I want to be the sigh

That slides between your lips

I want to be the rhythm

That guides your bucking hips

Say my name

say my name

say my name

One step at a time right?

Fuck it

Just come over tonight

Just drive over to my place

Just let me wrap my thighs around your

Face

There a chemistry between you and me

That should result in you

Being on your knees

Dinner dessert and you

You know what we should do

Break a bottle on a ship

Cut a ribbon

Shit

Let's christen every surface

When you climax

Your vibrato is perfect

One step at a time right?

Fuck it

Just come over tonight

Pull your pants down

Get on your hands and knees

Baby please

I need to taste

What you made for me

wishing well

when the air gets heavy
and i forget how to breathe
i take walks along the sea
there's a thicket of mango trees
where i go to dream of you and me
dreams i know will never come true
like 24 hours alone with you
or a place where we can be free
and for a little while you only belong to me
i close my eyes surrounded by island flowers
and i go to a place that's completely ours
a cabin up on a hill hugging the shore
a cobble path leading up to a white wooden door
and the sun is just starting to rise
a sweep of pink and orange decorating the sky
i'm a mess of anticipation and suspense
until i find you leaning against the backyard
fence
you smile and there's a bird where my heart used
to be
and its wings are beating furiously
"i've been waiting for you," you tell me
"did you make a wish to be with me?"
"yes," i hiss and then I'm touching your lips
spoiled for choice i settle for a kiss

"baby, baby, please forgive me for this"
it's tentative and soft at first
and then appreciation morphs to thirst
i open my mouth and push my tongue inside
our tongues press together and i hear you sigh
i move you closer to me, my hands on your
waist
i'm already drunk on the way your spit tastes
all hesitation and resolve fades
and your fingers begin to undo my braids
i hate wasting time so i guide you indoors
and we're stumbling across the wooden floor
you take off my hoodie and i undo your jeans
for us i want nothing but air in between
but when you're topless i lose my composure
your tits are out and i'm dazed in exposure
you chuckle and ask me "do you like what you
see?"
when i nod you reply "wait til you're inside of
me"
and then we're in bed and my mouth is full
your nipples are a feast, your breasts a handful
through the open window i hear ocean waves
crash
as i put two in your pussy and one in your ass
you're dripping wet and your juices are coating
me
and to the soundtrack of your moans i take you
rhythmically

in return you pet every inch of me you can reach
and i indulge in dessert with my face between
your knees
it takes us a while to get back on our feet
we have to keep touching because it's necessity
midday we go down to the shore for a stroll
but even out of the house we have little control
at one point you pull me out in to the sea
with water up to our calves, your request-
"finger me"
back inside drying off in the kitchen
watching you eat chocolate i find my religion
i bend down before you, worship you openly
i'm in love, fully, wholly, irrevocably
when it's dark again we lay a blanket in the sand
i tease you to weeping with the fingers of my
right hand
then cuddling after you finally ask me
"how much longer do i have with you Baby?"
"how long did they give us this time?"
"how long do I get to have you as mine?"
the sun sets slow behind the hill of our heaven
i have a sudden confession, your possesion my
obsession
for just a few more moments it's you and me
and i know that this is how it's supposed to be
where we're together in our cabin by the sea
and i'm free and your free to grow old with me
you hushes my sobs with your lips on mine

and remind me again, "we'll have this next time"
twilight becomes dusk which becomes night
and yeah, i'm panicking but i pretend i'm alright
your voice is soft when you say
"i need you to tell me all my favorite things,
okay?"
"i want you to keep saying them until the end"
"that way you feel them when we're back to just
friends"
i tell you "i love you so much, it's you that i
adore
"yesterday i loved you less and tomorrow i will
love you more"
all around us the beach grass, the dark crashing
waves
fuck i just want you to stay
i just want you to stay
but a wish come true is only a daydream
even when i feel you pumping through my veins
when reality comes and tears us apart
in your chest beats my thundering heart
even though we've accepted our situation
masturbation becomes our salvation
the weight of the world comes down on my
shoulders
but the fire between us endlessly smolders
a hope clings to the ribs in my chest
and my desire for you never gets any less
so when the air gets too heavy

and i forget how to breathe
i take walks along the sea
and i go to that thicket of mango trees
and i spend some time dreaming of you and me
and though i know wishes can't come true
you came to ME because i wished for YOU

wick

to express how i feel-
there is a candle and there is a flame
i am neither
i am the wick
between passion and pain
love is explicit
and exploitation is abundant
i am tired and dry
yet i remain hers and she remains his
so nothing is really mine
i am passionate and sultry
but my sex appeal does not offer hope
because i know in the end when she leaves me
i'll be reduced to nothing but a burning rope

wilde

i think that it will rain forever
that i will drown from missing you
Wilde says we're all in the gutter
well i was in heaven when i was fucking you

i think i will drink myself to death in this bar
if it will ease the pain of missing you
Wilde say that some of us are looking at stars
and there were stars in your eyes when i was
kissing you

my heart is sick and i know i will die from this
illness
fucking, kissing, loving and missing you
Wilde says memory is the diary that we carry
about with us
no matter how hard i try i can't stop loving you

Wilde says experience is simply the name we
give our mistakes
but i can't let go now so i guess this is just how
my heart breaks

dinner plans

tonight
as long as everything goes alright
i'm going to be meeting your parents
and due to the fact that i have some anxiety
i've devised a few plans you see
when we're at dinner with your family
in the suffocating heterosexual sea
of a restaurant i cannot afford
two artists, one mechanic and a lifetime member
of the PTO board
we'll pretend we're living in an alternate reality
where you're not dating me
we'll pretend that you are straight
and i am straight
and we smile and sip our waters straight
and we'll pretend that we're just friends
and in addition to friends we'll also pretend
that my tongue hasn't been in your mouth
and we'll definitely pretend is hasn't gone farther
south
but it'll just be an act we put on for them
because the entire time i'll be teasing your skin
with my right hand on your knee
the even pressure of my palm creating a soft heat
my petting will be so subtle

that you'll have no rebuttle
and you'll almost forget i'm touching you
and so at first, eye contact will be easy with your
dad
when he tells us about the day that he's had
and without effort we'll laugh at your mother's
jokes
and appreciate her corny euphemisms
and forget momentarily this afternoon's orgasms
but i'll be there to remind you
because just before we leave to meet them
i intend on fucking you
i'll have you pinned against the bathroom door
and then your ass will be on the hallway floor
then on your hands and knees in my bed
and finally your thighs on either side of my head
you'll be serenading me with moans
embracing me in pheromones
all the way up until eight
and then you'll starting saying that we were
going to be late
for my introductory dinner date
so we'll hurry to get there
and hurry to eat
as i get you squirming in your dining rom seat
everything will go on with no one the wiser
until just after we are served the appetizer
the fingers of my right hand
will curl around the hem of your dress

and immediately you'll feel wetness
as i drag the fabric up your thighs
my knuckles will brush your skin
and send shivers up and down your spine
and at that point what can i do
but continue lifting and revealing more of you
i'll uncover the tight band of your thong
and it'll feel too good to be wrong
so subtle the widening of your eyes
as my middle finger teases
you'll shiver in reply
and when i pull the edge of your underwear to
one side
and i make one long tantalizing swipe
you'll be desperate to remain silent
and not express the moan hidden behind your
lips
you'll try really hard to ignore the fact that i'm
doing this
but you won't be able to
and you'll whimper as i play with you
you'll whisper, one lifted eyebrow
"not here Baby. go to the bathroom- NOW"
then moments will tick by and then i'll stand up
my heart thundering with the tension built up
i'll tell your parents that i will be right back,
excuse me
and your parents will have no reason to do
anything but smile and nod at me

because you're really good at pretending to be
straight
but you're really bad at trying to wait
so you don't leave enough of a gap
between my hand in your lap
and slipping into the stall to be with me
directing my hand to your center
and begging to be taken by me
so you'll ride my fingers,
biting your lip
one hand over your mouth
my middle finger on your clit
your brow will furrow
the deeper i burrow
and you'll lean your head back
to stave off the attack
of the arousal that comes with your sexual need
as you keep rocking your hips desperate to
please
our sex will become a song we sing
your guiding hips lyrics
my pumping fingers the second string
but as your spiraling orgasm
follows your moans in chorus
someone will come inside looking for us
at first we'll think it's someone other
but then we'll see her shoes and realize it's your
mother
she'll tell us she's come to make sure we're okay

because it's been fifteen minutes that we've been
away
so i'll smooth your dress and step out to greet her
as you compose yourself i'll distract her
i'll tell your mother that you have a stomach bug
and i'll keep my glistening fingers out of sight
so that the only thing she'll ask is if you're
alright
i'll insist that you are
that you're just feeling a little nauseous
i'll tell her i have to take you home
and she won't argue
she'll just make me promise not to leave you
alone
so we'll go and say goodbye to your dad
and he will suggest you lie down and get some
rest
he'll express pleasantries so unsuspecting
and i'll try not to feel like i'm disrespcting
as my hand secretly strokes your ass
but i know you don't care one way or another
because your legs are still shaking
as you're hugging your mother
so when we'll turn to go
you'll sashay away real slow
and i'll follow close behind
all sorts of naughty things on my mind
we'll go to my car
which isn't parked far

and i'll go right back to touching you
i'll have my hands on you the entire time i'm
escorting you
one hand on the wheel the other between your
thighs
and as i stomp the gas pedal
you'll feel so alive
and i'll laugh because it's funny
that you're dad suggested you go lie down
because i intend on lying you down
right after i take your clothes off
kiss every inch of your skin
i'll bite and lick and suck you in
because i'd rather eat you than filet mignon
because the juices you pour in my mouth
are more exquisite than salade niçoise
and taste better than cabernet sauvignon
and the way we will drag our knives
through our steaks
will never compare to the way i will drag my
tongue across your slit
and the manner in which you dab your mouth
with your napkin
is not even slightly similar to how i will lift my
face from it
after i eat, using the back of my hand to get your
cum off my chin
right before your coo to me, "again, again.."
because your parents

i'm sure
are lovely people
but hearing all about the latest church gossip
will remind me about what it is that i like to
worship
and i would much rather
have you draped over me
cussing me out
as you're cumming for me
but i promised i'd go
and so we will go
give your dad our attention
offer your mother our laughter
but just know that i intend on taking you after
and i'll pretend that we're just friends
as i sip my water
but you'll know and i'll know
that i'm actively giving it to their daughter

no funny business

one hundred years of solitude
and then just as long in your arms
an impenetrable fortress of melancholia
reduced to rubble by your cazadorian charm
i have been so many places, but never lived
your necromancy lifted me from my grave
after a night of endless love making
you're getting dressed and asking me to behave
and in the afterglow of our rendezvous
knowing just a few moments ago you were mine
i accept that we have prior engagements to
attend
and very quickly, we're running out of time
so i'm lost in thought watching you move about
the room
knowing that this is all we are
but feeling my heart swell with adoration
in the radiance of my fallen star
i try my best not to cry in front of you
knowing we'll love again one day
for now all we can do is share a kiss
then you're gone and i'm not okay
it's beyond painful to step away from what is
real
and return to my solitude for a while

when i replay every fucking moment of us
i try to be chill but that's not my style
i'm dramatic when it comes to you
you consume my thoughts in my stillness
your glistening eyes, your pouting lips
trying to get ready "no funny business"
meaningless days, an almost never-ending haze
sprinkled with little moments of light
your face, your voice, your contagious laughter
the wings of my pounding heart taking flight
through the years, we weave in and out of each
other's lives
nothing about us or the way we feel fades away
the passage of time is absolutely irrelevant
because even when you leave me- i know you'll
always stay

as one sees the sun

i went down, trying not to look long at you as
though you were the sun
it was four o'clock and i was conscious that my
heart was beating fast
i was well dressed, my hat shining in the bright
sunlight
i saw you as one sees the sun, without looking

it was four o'clock and i was conscious that my
heart was beating fast
it was a sunny, frosty day and joy and terror
gripped my heart
i saw you as one sees the sun, without looking
you were a smile that brightened everything
around

it was a sunny, frosty day and joy and terror
gripped my heart
i was well dressed, my hat shining in the bright
sunlight
you were a smile that brightened everything
around
i went down, trying not to look long at you as
though you were the sun

the cottage of the wishing well

i will dream and go now,
to the cottage of wishing well
where i hide my sweetest treat
the angel of meadowsweet
with her honey eyes
and her decadent thighs
in the sunshine i will sing her praises
the second i have her beneath me, naked
and then under the ebony blanket of night
i will continue to bask in her holy light
the intellectual goddess beside the sea
who spends every moment loving me
i will dream and go now
to the cottage of wishing well
where rose bushes lead up to our door
and our souls are entertwined evermore
outside we have rocking chairs and windchimes
and up the cream colored stones, ivy climbs
white linen and driftwood is the interior decor
in our cottage by the new england seashore
a wicker couch, a crocheted quilt
wrapped up in the fantasy we built
i will dream and go now,
to the cottage of wishing well

where we can actually be together
in reality we cannot love
but in our cottage
our this is forevr

slanted rain

i took note of the angle
the angle of the slanted rain
on the balcony
the balcony of your brooklyn apartment
there was a curtain of precipitation around us
as we sat back
we sat back against the brick exterior wall
i watched you gaze out at the cityscape's horizon
the sudden strike of lightning
flashing in your eyes
your bottom lip was a soft pout
a soft pout that i longed to touch
i asked you what was on your mind
a deep cavernous thunder engulfed us
engulfed us in its cacophony
i could feel the tension rising
i could feel the pressure building
you spoke of trivial things
you spoke of things like work and bills
my eyes darted along your profile
my heart was pounding in my chest
my skin was tingling with anticipation
i inquired if that was all
you met my gaze
you met my gaze with your soft brown eyes

your soft brown eyes were dark with the storm
you told me you were trying to decide
you were trying to decide if this was right
we existed
we existed in that instance like two people
like two people preparing to jump
standing on on a cliff preparing to jump
we'd arrived at the climax of what had been
we'd arrived at the climax of what would be
i took your face in my hands
i took your face in my hands and brought you to
me
i pushed my lips against yours and you leaned in
to me
your cheek was warm beneath my palm
you whimpered
you whimpered when your bottom lip slipped
between my teeth
we gravitated towards one another
your breath was hot in my mouth
our tongues lashed together
lashed together in suffering agony
your hands clutched my hips
your fingernails dug into my skin
your mouth was sweet
your tongue was soft
your lips were sticky and wet
i tangled one hand in your hair
i had a deep pressing urge

a deep pressing urge to have more of you
we broke for air
we broke for intermission
i took note of the angle of the slanting rain
and then we went inside

pavlov

considering the fact that i am pavlov
you are a salivating dog
i will ring the bell of arousal
and cum will run down your thighs

you are a salivating dog
it will be easier to clean you up
when cum runs down your thighs
if you wear a dress tonight

it will be easier to clean you up tonight
when i ring the bell of arousal
if you wear a dress tonight
considering the fact that i am pavlov

seven days

I'll follow my backpack marker on my map to
get back to you if we get separated

these people i've stumbled across
in the post apocalyptic darkness
served a purpose for a while
but eventually became a burden
they are rusted scrap metal
picked up from a rubbish pile
they plant fibers punched from the earth
candy tin cans found in a hollow tree stump
and tungsten trophies contained in wall safes
but you aren't merely a trinket
that i'd stick in a secure wooden safe
i'd make sure to always stick you in my hotbar
because i don't know if you're aware
but you are ever useful
and damn near crucial in the life i live now
you are a Kevlar helmet
salvaged from an untouched weathered sports
bag
that i found lying in the middle of the snow
between two blueberry bushes
beside a birds nest containing 27 feathers
no

you are a can of miso soup
a bowl of venison stew
five jars of bottled water
and a blue berry pie
found in a dirty blue purse
by the side of a gravel road
no
you are a full stack of wooden frames
hidden in the second to last cabinet
of the make-shift shelter in the woods
that was mostly torn down
and totally abandoned
no
you are a fucking sniper rifle
and seventy-three 762mm bullets
looted from a dropped backpack
at the top of the apartment complex
in the city rock biome
behind the boarded up city hall
and you'll get me through the hordes
and together we'll take on the undead
the decayed cheerleaders and infected survivors,
the bloated walkers and frozen lumberjacks,
the frostbitten workers and frigid hunters
the burn victims and crawlers
the festering corpses and plagued nurses,
and a pack of fucking zombie dogs
we'll raid the Shotgun Messiah
the Born & Noble

the Working Stiffs
and if you start to break down
I'll craft a weapon repair kit
out of cloth fragments
metal strips
and oil
and we'll build a shelter
out of chrysanthemum stained planks
and even if the zombies take me down
don't worry darling
i'll respawn on my bedroll
and we'll climb into the attic
crouch on the back wall
between an empty bookcase
and an air conditioning unit
and we will wait it out til morning
because a supply drop will come in seven days
and if you're with me
i know i will make it

limitless

her form is limitless to me

because when our gazes meet

i crawl through her

and she extends on forever all around me

holding me within and without her

but my fingertips trace her contours

like coloring book outlines

and i use anything

to fill her with shades of passion

sometimes absolutely emptying myself

just to pour into her such intense hues

that the vibrance of them

makes me temporarily look away

to keep from being intially blinded

by the glory that is her radiance

and for a second i am spent

i am less me

than i was

before i touched her

barely a shell of curious wanting fervor

that could surely never be pleased

but when i look into her toasted caramel irises

her body entwined with mine

and undulating directly parallel to my own

i am refilled instantaneously

what's more- there is no end

to the parabola that her back lifts into

as her mouth hangs open

and emits a myriad of husky breaths

and involuntary demands of

"touch me there" and

"don't stop"

but it's unimportant

because the pattern of pleasure

goes on unhindered

unchanged

and her legs wrap around me

forcing me ever closer

until i believe i am actually becoming her

and if i close my eyes for a moment

i will re-open them from her point of view

and see myself through her eyes

and be her

and feel be from my within

because in essence i am

we are one

and in the moment her eyes flash

and her lips curl

to reveal her pointed canine teeth

that she just recently had slicing

into the flesh of my shoulder

i decide that the love i feel for her

is not restricted to the thundering

of my pounding heart

but instead overflows completely

and is found in every inch of her skin

motion of her muscle

bead of her sweat

that collects

in the dip of her collar bones

and it is also found

in every release of her quiet whimpers

that she so politely gives me

right before her body collapses beside mine

and we await the coming rounds

that are only post-poned by the exhaustion

that ravages all of me

save for those same fingetips

that still glisten with wetness

but continue to trace those contours

because even in sleep i cannot

stop touching her

and so

much like her

and her unrestricted boundaries

of devotion

and desire

our very love

that fuels me

her

us

in union

is limitless

event horizon

Because I keep thinking about day one

And how absolute it was

I recall those six or seven hours

Before the entropy

I know that wasn't you

I paid for a show and became a conquest

I didn't fall; I dove

Now, a stain on the concrete

Thousands of feet below the apartment of my marriage

I can transmit insults your way

But it only hurts

The moment I met you I wanted to save you

And hurting you makes me feel like I failed

I love you but you mustn't fault for me for it

You are a galactic gravity swallowing mass

You suck the masculinity

The femininity

The personality

Out of everyone you've ever brushed past

In reality I stand clutching my chest

stumbling, pale and frail

Void of power

Because you are a succubus

With your beautiful canines

The feathers of your raven hair

Your long fingers and tapered legs

I can't really shake the burns

That your acid lips kissed onto my skin

The April sun made you appear innocent

You are young

You are dreadful

I thoroughly loathe you

Still, I unzip your jacket

Feel useless, wasted, tormented

By my fidelity

By your infidelity

You let your clothes fall to the floor

They crumple in a pile

Like my past life

My hopes and ambitions

My future

I am blowing in every direction

You are too pretty for me

I am too good for you

I just want to hold your hand you jerk

I have no self resistance

I'm existing in a sense of imbalance

Teetering on the edge of your event horizon

Struggling to keep from being pulled apart

Atom by atom

Stretched out like linguine

Gone forever in the black hole that is you

I am gravity

There is no escape

delicacy

This time the fiend was not dead
it bared its teeth as it raised its head
everyone lived again because of a curse
it was a highway to hell driven in a hearse
she lifted her chin and set her jaw
now her lover wasn't her lover at all
so she cocked her pistol as the sky began to fall
and she placed the barrel to her temple
being with her now was entirely simple
she would never be the one to kill her lover
but being together was a promise they'd made
one another
so as the zombie neared her hide-out
she pulled the trigger and blew her brains out
unfortunately there was no grand reunion or
gospel
a love life between zombies is entirely
impossible
all there was was a grand feast
because her brains were a delicacy now that her
lover was a beast

listen

Listen very closely

Because I am not

Extremely good

At explaining things

And I know that you

Being the ever-thirsty

Insatiable

Girl that you are

That you will break this apart

And dissect meaning

From every word

But Baby

The sun doesn't shine

Very brightly

In the winter

But YOU do

And I have the hardest time

Staying warm

Except for when your arms

Cloak my shoulders

And your indulgent kisses

Pepper my jaw

And your fingers dip

Into the collar of my shirt

And stroke so gently

That I forget your

Explicit intentions

And humbly relax

Drifting into pure

Innocent delight

Because Darling

I adore you

And your petite sighs

Your miniature whimpers

Your tiny moans

And as I plummet into slumber

Every evening I spend missing you

I allow your affection

To serve as my blanket

And even when I close my eyes

You fill me up inside

And I can't fathom

The notion

Of not being your world

So let's discover ourselves together

Empathy

Sympathy

You are my sky

And I swear I soar

In your lovely russet eyes

And yes

I know you require time

But I am not embellishing

When I say would wait an epoch

If it meant even a twinkling moment

As your girl

Still, regardless

I'll be here waiting

When you're absolutely ready

to stand by my side

I'll just swoop behind you

Hold you up

And show you what it is

To really be alive

Angel

The golden light of morning streams in

Cascades across you, sparkling on your skin

After a night of lovemaking you're peacefully
asleep

And I'm blissful beside you just watching you
breathe

My fingers caress the soft skin of your breasts

Then slip easily between your thighs without
protest

With my right hand between your knees

With an even pressure I push and a gentle touch
I tease

With a soft murmur you stir as I begin to pet
your center

then your warm caramel eyes flutter open as I
finally enter

Accompanied by your sighs we dance back into passion

Your furrowed eyebrows mirroring your satisfaction

And as your sweet whimpers turns to purring

I feel a curious sensation deep within me, stirring

I become lost in memory of meeting you

Of knowing you, wanting you and absolutely needing you

From the moment I first saw you I was absolutely stricken

With this all encompassing lovesick condition

It wasn't anything akin to simple infatuation

It was a hungry, gnawing, aching, desperation

And like a fever, you spread through me completely

When you gazed in my eyes, when you smiled
so sweetly

I didn't understand it but I felt you crawling
through my soul

And without thinking I surrendered full control

Surely some could say I'm crazy, or call me a
fool

But I didn't need you to conquer me- I just
wanted you to rule

You see, being around you in the beginning was
painful

Because I was a mortal and you were an angel

And I didn't think myself worthy of your
attention

This bond between us was beyond
comprehension

And the magnetism between us only promised
obsession

So I didn't fight it when I felt your possession

And you didn't fight it when I got you undressed

Kissed your soft lips, let intimacy do the rest

And now my fingers are deep and you're
panting

And I can't help but find your sounds enchanting

And when your lip twitches I can't look away

You're addicting to me when you want it this
way

One end is the beginning of another climax

You can't stop I can't stop; neither of us can
relax

For now we're back in our cottage together

And you know and I know this moment can't
last forever

So as the golden light of morning streams in

You let me kiss and lick every inch of your skin

And as the morning drifts on into the day

You're holding me tighter and begging me to stay

But we have jobs and families and lives to live too

But living only counts when I'm living with you